Our Community

Librarians Help

by Dee Ready

Consulting editor: Gail Saunders-Smith, PhD

CAPSTONE PRESS
a capstone imprint

Pebble Books are published by Capstone Press,
1710 Roe Crest Drive, North Mankato, Minnesota 56003
www.capstonepub.com

Library of Congress Cataloging-in-Publication Data
Ready, Dee.
  Librarians help / by Dee Ready.
      pages cm. — (Pebble Books. Our Community Helpers)
  Includes bibliographical references and index.
  Summary: "Simple text and photographs describe librarians and their role in the
community"— Provided by publisher.
  ISBN 978-1-62065-084-4 (library binding)
  ISBN 978-1-62065-847-5 (paperback)
  ISBN 978-1-4765-1719-3 (ebook pdf)
1. Librarians—Juvenile literature. 2. Libraries—Juvenile literature. I. Title.
  Z682.R43 2013
  020.92—dc23   2012038073

Note to Parents and Teachers

The Our Community Helpers set supports national social studies
standards for how groups and institutions work to meet individual
needs. This book describes and illustrates librarians. The images
support early readers in understanding the text. The repetition of
words and phrases helps early readers learn new words. This book
also introduces early readers to subject-specific vocabulary words,
which are defined in the Glossary section. Early readers may need
assistance to read some words and to use the Table of Contents,
Glossary, Read More, Internet Sites, and Index sections of the book.

Printed in the United States of America in Stevens Point, Wisconsin.
092012   006937WZS13

Table of Contents

What Is a Librarian?

Librarians help people find information. They help people find books, magazines, websites, and other materials.

Some librarians work in schools. They help students find information for reports. They help teachers find materials for lessons.

Other librarians work in public libraries. These libraries are open to anyone. They have materials and computers for people to use.

Librarians work other places.
Some work in hospitals, law
offices, or other workplaces.
Some drive bookmobiles
to towns without libraries.

What Librarians Do

Librarians teach people how to find answers to questions. They also help people find materials to read or watch for fun.

Librarians buy materials and plan events for the library. They might do story hours or book clubs. They plan summer reading programs.

Tools

Librarians use computers.
A computer catalog shows
all the materials in a library.
Librarians use it to find
materials for people.

Librarians use computers in other ways. They help people use online encyclopedias. Scanners connected to computers check out materials.

Librarians Help

Librarians help everyone in a community find books, movies, and other materials. Librarians help people learn and have fun.

Glossary

bookmobile—a van or truck that holds library materials that can be checked out there, rather than going to a library

catalog—a list of items

community—a group of people who live in the same area

lesson—a set of skills or facts taught during a specific amount of time; teachers plan lessons for class

materials—items that people may look at in libraries or check out of libraries; books, videos, and magazines are library materials

public—having to do with people in general

scanner—a machine that moves a beam of light over a code and sends the code information to a computer

website—a place on the Internet

Read More

Ames, Michelle. *Librarians in Our Community.* On the Job. New York: PowerKids Press, 2010.

Crabtree, Marc. *Meet My Neighbor, the Librarian.* Meet My Neighbor. New York: Crabtree Publishing Company, 2012.

Kenney, Karen Latchana. *Librarians at Work.* Meet Your Community Workers! Edina, Minn.: Magic Wagon, 2010.

Internet Sites

FactHound offers a safe, fun way to find Internet sites related to this book. All of the sites on FactHound have been researched by our staff.

Here's all you do:

Visit *www.facthound.com*

Type in this code: 9781620650844

Check out projects, games and lots more at
www.capstonekids.com

Index

Word Count: 177
Grade: 1
Early-Intervention Level: 17

Editorial Credits
Gillia Olson, editor; Gene Bentdahl, designer; Eric Manske, production specialist

Photo Credits
Alamy: Corbis Flirt/Jim Craigmyle, 14; Capstone Studio: Karon Dubke, 4, 12, 16; Corbis: Blend Images/Sam Bloomberg-Rissman, 6; NBAE via Getty Images: Layne Murdoch, 10; Newscom: Digital Ligh/Richard Hutchings, 18, OJO Images, 20; Shutterstock: Blend Images, 8; SuperStock Inc.: Blend Images, cover